Tearstained Alchemy
A Collection of Poetry and Prose

By Daniela Stankovic

ISBN: 978-1-7368240-0-9

Cover Artwork by: Molly O'Day (*Instagram: @modaisy)*

for anyone
who has
ever thought
of giving
up hope,
this is
for you

tearstained alchemy is the
seemingly magical process of
transforming tears into
the words of your soul

I once knew this girl who lost herself in a not so perfect relationship.
She was young when they met and she thought this was the best love she'd ever get.
Countless times she would justify all the nights he made her cry.
It wasn't that he was a bad guy, he just didn't love her the way she needed, and he wouldn't try.
Blinded by what she believed she wanted, she missed all the warning signs.
The passion they shared burned a bright, hot red. She found herself intrigued by his flames.
She insisted that this inferno of a man was the only man she would ever love.
Her life changed the day she opened her eyes to everything that he had set ablaze in her world.
For years they'd dance in and out of a relationship with one another.
Every time he'd change his mind about what he wanted from her.
She convinced herself that he truly loved her despite what he showed her.
She gave and gave all the love and compassion she had stored away in her heart.
She could never shake this nagging, worrisome feeling that their love was falling apart.
Many tearstained nights were spent alone in her room— trying to figure out why he didn't love her the same way she loved him.
She truly believed she could never get over someone she loved so much… to the point where she got stuck.

1

Years and years flew by before she would even try to let go.

She was not the type of person to give up on the things she loved, however, it became apparent that the more she held on to this broken love, the more she was hurting herself in the end.

One day she finally found the courage to tell herself that the painful cycle needed to stop and she allowed herself to begin the one thing she deemed impossible.

She started to move on.

More importantly, she found the love she was searching for in the one place she never thought to look... within herself.

I want to help every broken, beaten, and battered person out there. I want to let every human know that my heart is always open and I will never judge. I want those who feel like they need a little extra love to know that there is nothing wrong with them. And that you, your physical being, must absolutely love yourself.

No matter how bad things are, there will always be something great waiting for you with open arms. I need you to know that you are not alone in the way you are feeling. A lot of people go through tough times and even though you may not know it, they are constantly fighting battles.

You will overcome your demons. You will become such an amazing person; you just have to believe in you. It's hard, but darling, it's worth it. I promise; life will be wonderful if you let us (you and I, both) believe in you.

I understand how ridiculous it may sound for me to say that I know what you're feeling because no one but you truly knows… however, I have been through a whirlpool of disappointments; I have drowned in all depths of pain. So, although it may not be exactly the same, I know what it's like to be in need. I especially know what it's like to feel trapped with nowhere to turn.

I have decided I don't want anyone else to ever feel as alone as I have. I don't want anything I have experienced to be felt by anyone else. I want those who are scared and hurting to know that they can, and they will get better.

I want to pull every single person who feels like they are laying in the gutter, up and out of it. I want the people who think that they are worthless to stop for a moment, place their hand over their heart, and just breathe. Inhale. Exhale.

Then I want you to promise (to me, to yourself, or to whomever you wish) that you will not do anything to harm yourself, or disrupt that perfect little breathing pattern; okay? I get that everything is dark and cold, and you feel like giving up. But, you can't, sweetheart, not yet. You have so much more to live for. So much left to experience.

I want to let you in on a little theory I have: those who are facing continuous setbacks are supposed to. The science behind that theory is…irrelevant. I do believe that you were given the ultimate gift: the ability to survive.

You are much stronger than the average person. If you can make it through the struggles you are facing now, then you are a superhero in my book. I think, further down the line, you'll find out exactly why you needed to endure so much pain. We will become unstoppable individuals, we just can't give up yet.

welcome to
heaven on
earth —
i mean
my heart;
the warmest
place you'll
love to
grow

i
ask
that
you
tread
the
waters
of
my
heart
lightly;
couldn't
risk
letting
you
drown

you are a
m a s t e r p i e c e
i'd like to
hang up
in the
museum
of my
heart

if i had to paint
a picture of what
loving you is like

it'd be a still night
on the shore
underneath
the glistening
moonlight

up above the sky
would glow with
dancing stars

the waves would
ripple across
the canvas

our love
as endless
as the ocean

if i could
end
every night &
begin
every morning
with you

                by
                my
                side

every single
day would
be the
greatest
of my
life

sitting on the
edge of the sand
as the waves
greet me at my feet

dancing barefoot
through an empty
field with sweet
summer rain
pouring down
on me

laying on delicate grass
gazing up at
the glistening
night sky

falling asleep
entangled in
your embrace
as the calmness of
your breath
washes over
me

being next to you causes my heart to race
chills trickle all down my spine
the second your lips approach my face
your kiss is a sweet wine
i'm addicted to your taste
i cherish every memory we make
time spent with you is never a waste
the bond between us will not easily break
in your strong embrace i feel most protected
the fire of your love keeps me warm inside
our souls are so deeply connected
it's like a burst of magic when they collide
i never imagined i could love someone like this
you changed my life for the better
loving you is pure bliss

(i think i'll leave this note on your sweater)

i want to be
the person that
gets to spend
forever
loving you

memorizing
every inch of
your enchanting
soul

running my
fingers down
your past

lighting up
the darkest
corners of your
marvelous mind

dancing with
the dangerous
demons that keep you
up all night

i want
nothing more
than to be
forever yours

you are the blood
pulsating through my
veins

you are the sweet
melody humming in
my ears

you are the tears
shed upon my
pillow late
at night

you are the brightest
star shining through
my darkest
night

you are the air
filling my lungs
when i couldn't
figure out how to
breathe

you are the stars,
the sky & the moon
creating the most
astonishing view

i wrapped
a hammock
around both
sides of
your heart
& made it
my home

i want
to pour
my love
into your
broken soul
and watch
as it
flows into
the cracks
slowly making
you whole

you have
awakened
the happiest
version of
myself
one i
never
fathomed
could survive
inside of
me

the wretched
darkness
that once
consumed
my fiery
soul
has been
replaced
with the
sweetest
 light

your
soft
touch
on
my
sensitive
skin
sends
a thousand
lightning
bolts
rippling
within

all versions of me
past,
present,
future
can agree;

you are the
greatest
thing
to ever
happen
to me

last night
i dreamt
of you

you looked
beautiful
as you
always do

your smile
warmed my
heart

made me
forget
how long
we've been
apart

i love
the way
your lips
taste
i'm addicted
to the
little things

when you
run your
fingers through
your
perfect hair

oh, and those
dimples
when you
smile,
drives my
heart
completely wild

cherry kisses

my tongue
craves
your sweet
taste

my refreshing
summertime
snack

your love
staining
my lips
deep red

like the
fire
burning in
my heart
for you

the
chaos
we
create
has
a
sweet
addicting
taste

your love burrowed
its way through
the concrete walls
guarding my heart

tore them down
and made a
home out of
my chest

year after year
your love grew
and grew until
one day
you decided
my love was
just too much
for you

now i'm left
cleaning up
the mess
of my
uninvited guest

i am entangled
in my love for you

slowly, but effectively
strangling myself
with the love that
was meant for you

drowning in
my feelings for you

every thought
of you comes in
like a
treacherous wave
engulfing me

all the memories
flood in and
i suffocate
reminding me
that the only

way out
is by
letting go
of this
sinking ship

i keep falling into the pattern of you
spilling my love messily over you
i get sucked into the comfort of us to the point where i get stuck
i continuously am picking myself up, but never high enough to get
over you
this false love we've got is intoxicating
one moment with you is more than enough to get addicted
the longer i stay around you, the harder it will be to leave, and it's hard
enough as it is
i've come to the conclusion that we've always been the same yet
wildly different
you're the sun; **boisterous and bright**, seeking attention but only to
hurt those who want to get close
i am the moon; *soft, mellow and ever-changing*
we both belong in the sky, but you've got the day and i dance with the
night

feeling defeated
by the day,
she crawls
into bed
with tears
in her eyes
and a
heavy heart
she looks
up to the
sky
apologizes to
the moon
for
giving up
so soon
and cries
until she
can no
longer
hold open
her eyes

i will always
love you
not because
i am some
irrational
or
deranged woman
but because
throughout our
time
you earned my
love and
unfortunately
for me
that just
doesn't vanish
when you
do

insanity —
doing the same thing
again and again, and
expecting a different
result
that's how the past
few years of my
life have been;
trying
to heal myself
while not changing
a single thing
loving
someone who
wasn't sure of
their feelings for me
giving
parts of my soul
to people who
weren't ready for it
trusting
that things would
just work themselves
out in the end

i learned the hard way; change is absolutely necessary for growth

compelled by
the darkness
within

losing faith
in finding the
right light
one that is
strong enough
to win

these demons
wake in the
midst of night
lightly pulling
on the strings
of your heart

tightly gripping
the throat of
your soul
squeezing out
false emotions that
rip you apart

all to let you know
you will never
be whole

i'm the
human equivalent
of a
hurricane

wreaking havoc
on everyone
whose life
i pass
through

ruining
everything
i can
wrap my
stormy
hands
around

they run
for cover
when they
see me

your words don't
have the same
weight they
used to

i've managed
to escape
your lethal
hold

the death grip
you had
on my
soul

i'm finally
free

time to
spread my
wings and
be me

there are layers
to everything you feel
you hide your pain
under temporary satisfaction

hoping it will
eventually disintegrate and
no longer be
a thought in your mind

the pain is still there
wallowing in the corners
of your subconscious

waiting for its
chance to break out
of the pandora's box
that you tried
so hard to
forget about
while
it tried so hard
to claw its
way out

picture this:

an empty sensation
that leaves you
so hollow
you are clutching
your sides
gasping for
air that can't
fill your lungs
quick enough

a feeling so
powerful
it pierces a hole
straight through
your soul

a deep kind
of pain that keeps
you up all night
forcing you
to search for
the parts
of you
that *could* be
missing

my
skin
aches
for
your
tender
touch

.

i have become
like a memory;
tucked away
in the corners
of your mind

the thought
of me fades
with each
day and
soon i
will be
completely
forgotten

forgotten
like all
the lies
that have
fallen from
your deadly
tongue

"you mean so much to me."

"i promise i'll never leave."

meaningless phrases
burned holes
into my
soul

damaging me
forever

the day we met
you engraved your name
deep into my brain

everyday since you left
i've been drowning in
the pain of missing
your lips,
craving your strong
hands on my hips

i grip the
memories of
us so tightly,
refusing to let
you slip through
my fingers

even though
you've already
left long ago

those who say
"i'll never leave you"
are typically the
first to go

you cling to
a small
ray of
hope,
believing they
will be
different

it always ends
up hurting
the same
the minute
they turn
to walk
away

life is a
never-ending
cycle of
w a t c h i n g
those you
love most
l e a v e,
waiting for
new ones to
take their place
and learning
to love yourself
in between

drip.

                drip.

                                drip.

there go my feelings
pouring out of me
helplessly
like raindrops
falling from
heavy clouds
i'm drenched now
saturated in pain,
dripping with love,
slipping on spilled regret
content and confusion
wash over me like
an enormous wave
drowning in despair
choking on my anxiety
searching, frantically
for a way out of
my own head

love will *rip* you apart

and love is the only way to
pull yourself back together

although you'll never
be quite the same again

you'll find yourself
running your fingers
over the scars
it left behind

chasing the memories
you hold deep in
your heart

praying to have it
once again

they say:
the eyes are
the window to
the soul
that must be
why every
single time
i look into
a mirror
i get chills
down my
spine
and tears
immediately
fill my eyes

i am forced
to see all of
the brokenness
within me

broken
people
find
solace
in
the
holes
of
each
other

i fear
there
will
never
be
a love
strong
enough
to mend
the
gaping
hole
in my
heart

i spend
most of
my time
wrapped up
comfortably
in a
daydream
as a
means to
survive
the coldness
that is
reality

if i
don't come
back down
everything
around me
will come
crashing
down

i lost myself over a lilac lover turned liar.

it was easy to get caught up in those emerald green eyes that were bright enough to light up the night sky.

i would have curled up into your dimple and fallen asleep if i was small enough.

there is a tiny, almost unnoticeable aching in my heart that yearns for you.

it's going to be something i learn to live with or learn to ignore because i refuse to ever extend my heart out and reach for you again.

honestly, how many times can one person get burned by the same flame before realizing it's not an illusion, they're just that dangerous.

detrimental to my health and well being.

you always brought out the worst in me.

these are the things i need to remember whenever my heart tries to convince me that i miss you.

the version of you that i loved never truly did exist.

i had fallen in love with the idea of you i had conjured up in my mind; therefore there is nothing to miss.

sadness
swung
from
her
lips

delved
deep
into
her
soul
and
made
itself
at
home

free yourself
from people
who don't
spark joy
in your
heart
you're not
tethered to
anybody
break free
from society
and live
happily

my love for you
hangs on tightly

like a yellow-red
leaf clinging
desperately
to its branch
in the late
autumn breeze

and like a leaf
plunging rapidly
to the cold, hard
ground
all this love
for you will
eventually
come crashing
down

it will hurt
it might take
four seasons
to heal but just as
new leaves are born
with the spring
new love will
bloom again

there's so much darkness that it's so easy to get lost in it. you try so hard to see the light, that you look right past it. and when you don't have a safe place; someone you can turn to, that you trust, it gets hard to keep fighting. you get weary, beaten by time. nothing seems worthwhile anymore. happiness feels like a lifetime away. most people don't even notice you suffering; that every day you are alive, you're in a full on war with yourself.

but those scars you have, they're proof you survived and that you can make it through anything. you're a warrior. you kept going even when you didn't know your way. you kept fighting despite the inner voices that screamed "you should give up already." you lived through the war and now, Love, it's time to make peace with yourself. let the healing begin.

would you let me
hold you until
the aching in
your soul goes
away?

can i place my
lips on your
fears and kiss
them until they
dissipate?

if you let me,
i can show
you how to
annihilate all
that burning
hate

and we can create
a buoyant and
loving place for
your soul to
decorate

let
me
hold
your
heart
in
my
hands
i
promise
to
be
gentle
with
it

i feel for the people who don't
get along with the voice in
their head

those who are constantly
waging a war between
the good and the bad thoughts

the people who break day
simply because they fear dreaming

those who have to
face their demons alone

the people who
can no longer see
the light that supposedly
comes after this darkness

those searching for
a reason to keep on going
when every ounce
of their being is telling
them to give up already

for the people
who are like me

hope has a
tendency to be
elusive
keeping up with
her will be
exhausting
she'll make you
jump through all
kinds of
hoops
nothing will
ever seem
to be good
enough
to satisfy her
just as
you decide
you're ready
to give up,
that you
no longer
want to
play hope's
games

she reminds you just how much she's helped you grow

i will always love myself
i will always put myself first

i won't tolerate any form of disrespect
i will believe in myself, there is
no room for doubt

i won't allow anybody to treat
me poorly, myself included
i will stop to appreciate everything
about myself and my life

i will remind myself that i am
greater than everything
that has happened to me

i will remind myself no matter
how badly i want to give up,
i am not going to

sometimes we get so choked up by the uncertainty of love that we allow fear to present itself in our thoughts and actions. love and life are one in the same in regards to uncertainty. there is no guarantee that we will wake up the next morning, but our expectations lead us to believe that we will, and we live our lives barely acknowledging that uncertainty. so why shouldn't we do the same when it comes to love? why do we allow the uncertainty of a relationship allow us from enjoying the time we have together? one of the greatest pleasures in life is having someone to share our time with, so we need to stop trying to predict and control the future, and just simply appreciate the love you are experiencing in the moment. you can't live your life running away from a hypothetical.

don't believe
the vicious
lies
you tell
yourself

don't fall
for the
mirage
created by
your unhappy
mind

the only
way the
darkness
wins is
if it
remains
locked inside

everything changes
the moment
you decide to
love yourself

the world around
you gets brighter
your once heavy
heart feels lighter,
the holes in your soul
start to close and you
slowly begin to feel whole

leaving you to wonder
how was it that you
lived your life without
a love like this

i'm sorry
for ever doubting
all that you are capable of

i'm sorry
i tried so hard to
break your gentle spirit

i'm sorry
i never believed
in you the way i
needed to
or loved you
the way you deserved

i wish we
could start over,
make our relationship
right from the start

life doesn't work that way
so instead from this day
forward, i promise to
make everything up to you

hey!
just thought i'd remind you of what a great job you've been doing
lately. i know how hard it can get, but no one can do a better job at
being you! you're going to make it through and i hope you will be
proud of yourself too. you are truly mesmerizing; the way you keep
your head high despite the pain you hold in your heart and the tears
you refuse to let fall from your eyes. you are strong; you are persistent.
you will get out of this alive. strap up your combat boots and get ready
to take these demons to war. anyone who knows you can tell you that
these demons don't stand a chance against you and the artilleries you
have concealed in your heart.

be proud of who you are. no one else is able to replace you. the world
only has *o n e* you, appreciate that.
you are uniquely you.

take your hands
push them past
all that self-hatred
pull out the
friend that is
buried deep
within your
sweet, aching
soul

wrap them in
your arms
apologize for
mistreating them

show them
the love
they've been
missing out
on for
their whole
life

be kind to you.

show yourself the same compassion you show your best friend.

be there for yourself when it feels like there is no one else.

save yourself.

fix yourself.

be whole on your own.

make yourself happy.

learn how to love yourself in the way you wish every lover you ever had could.

whatever you do for yourself, make sure it is out of love.

be the person you need.

love who you are.

you are worthy.

be understanding.
be patient.
be kind.
have faith.
have hope.
believe.
dream.
love.
create.
trust.
learn.
grow.

the best advice
you'll ever
receive
take it, and
make it your
mission to truly
love all aspects
of who you
have the
potential
to be.

beauty emanates
from her
celestial being

a smile warmer
than the sun
shines from her lips

an ocean of hair
flows and waves
with each step
she takes

there's a twinkle
in her eyes
that dances like
the stars in
a night sky

today,
i learned
there **is**
a love
strong
enough
to pull
the two
halves of
my broken
heart
back together

we need more people who acknowledge their flaws
and yet still try to love themselves endlessly

it's time to start teaching each other
to unconditionally love

that it's okay to fall down,
to not be okay,
to need some time to
pick yourself back up

that breaking down is
a normal part of growing up

being hard on yourself
does nothing but beat you down
and stunt your growth

try not to place blame on you
there wasn't a single thing you
could do to prevent
the way life comes at you

just take it slow
i need you to know

life **will** get better

don't fall in love with an idea.

fall in love with the person who loves every part of you. the person who wants to understand you. the person who is willing to learn what makes you feel unstoppable in love.

you deserve someone who shows up for you, not someone who constantly disappoints and hurts you. your heart has been through more than enough pain, it is due for some tender love.

i hope you find someone who sweeps you off of your feet. someone who puts you first, makes you feel secure. someone who is proud to love you. you deserve better than being a well-kept secret. you need someone who will scream their love for you as loud as possible and who will stop at nothing to make you smile. someone that looks at you and sees the incredible soul that you are. you deserve to be praised. you deserve the best love that life has to offer, and you will get it.

the smallest
ray of
light
can make
the brightest
difference
when you've
been lost
in the
darkness

just a quick reminder:
you are worthy of love. you are so deserving of every magical thing
this life has to offer and more. your inner beauty shines brighter than
millions of stars. your light is unmatched; your soul radiates more love
than anything else. you are absolutely mesmerizing. the universe can't
believe someone with your magnetism actually exists. the people in
your life are like flowers and you're their sunshine; without you there
is no growth. never allow anyone to dim your magnificent light.
your essence is pure love and that is the only love you should accept.
you may not notice how much you mean, but i can promise you,
anyone who has had the pleasure of knowing you will agree that
you're just as important as the moon is to the night. you have a galaxy
inside of you.
please don't sell yourself short. there is not a single soul in the world
who can love like you.

please don't feel
like you need someone,
all you really need is yourself.
if you'd love yourself
as much as you
wanted to be loved
you'd never feel lonely again
in time all your emptiness
will fade away
and you'll be left
with a love that
radiates

you must be gentle,
caring, patient, and
understanding;
for healing takes time
don't forget to plant seeds
of love in your heart and
be sure to water them
regularly with compliments
and positive reinforcements
before you know it,
you will have yourself
a luscious garden
of self-love

some days,
i'll spend
hours
ripping out
old habits
and in the
holes
plant seeds
of self-love
into the garden of
my heart

other days,
i prance around
the same garden
wearing cleats
laced with
my old ways
destroying
all evidence
of self-love
in a
matter
of seconds

old habits might die hard, but i keep trying

i like the people society
considers to be damaged

they are truly fascinating
and the way they move
despite all the hurt
is captivating,
motivating

they are invincible,
though they might
not always see it

real life superheroes,
fighting the ultimate battle

not many understand how
much strength it takes to
make it through each day

i hope they believe me when i say
that i am proud of them
for not allowing
the darkness to win

An Open Letter to Anyone Who Has Ever Left My Life;

I want to start out by saying thank you. Thank you for coming into my life at the exact moment that you did. Thank you for all the wonderful memories you blessed my mind with. Thank you for teaching me the lessons I needed to learn. Thank you for loving me and showing me there is life beyond the pain. Thank you for teaching me that no matter how much love you put into something, there is always a chance it will go away. Thank you for being a part of me. Thank you for the growth you have provided me by leaving. Thank you, because without you, I wouldn't have became who I am today.

Next, I would like to apologize. I'm sorry if I ever made you feel like you were anything short of amazing. I'm sorry if I was not enough of a friend for you. I'm sorry if I was too much for you. I'm sorry if I ever said something that hurt you. I'm sorry if I came on too strong, or if I was distant. I'm sorry if I was too needy or clingy. I'm sorry if being around me was draining. I'm sorry if I pushed you away. I'm sorry if I ever caused you any kind of pain. I'm sorry if I left you hurt with questions unanswered. I'm sorry if I abandoned you. I am so truly sorry for doing anything that caused you the slightest bit of discomfort.

I wasn't me. I know that sounds like the greatest excuse of all time, but I truly mean it. The girl who was occupying my body for the last seven years was not me or anything I ever intended to be. You see, I was a product of years of repressed trauma and self-loathing, which lead to a depression greater than anything I've ever known. I was lost inside myself. The person who I felt like I had to be was nothing like the person I was or wanted to be. The worst part is, I was blind to what had taken over me.

I've been reflecting a lot lately and felt the need to make amends with the people who are no longer in my life. This may not reach every one of them. It might not even reach any of them, but it is something that I needed to get out of me.

One last thing. . . I wish you well in life. I want nothing more than for you to be truly happy. I hope you accomplish all you set out to do and overcome any obstacles that get in your way. You have the ability to be anything you want to be and I hope you never lose sight of that. I want you to live your best life. I want you to grow and be successful. I wish you the best of luck in everything you set out to do. I still care about you, even if I don't know you anymore.

Take Care of Yourself,
D.

a wound
on the
soul
takes
lifetimes
to heal

- remember to be patient with your healing process

i lace
my fingers
through hope

gripping
her hand
we walk

ready to
take on
anything
the day
attempts to
throw
our way

fantasies are
a beautiful
break from
a harsh
reality

be gentle with yourself. stand up for yourself and be the advocate you need. find your voice and scream your truth to the universe. don't let anyone invalidate your life experience. don't allow anyone to stifle your growth, even if that person is you. tell yourself that you **are** worthy and spend as much time as necessary proving it to yourself. i understand it's not an easy task, but it is important for you to at least try. also know; you might not immediately feel any different, but trust me when i say that *falling in love with yourself, respecting yourself, being there for yourself when you need it* will change your life. self-love is the most incredible love you'll ever know. nobody on this earth will ever love and care for you the way that you can. nothing feels better than saying, "you know what? i deserve this. i truly deserve the love i so desperately try to give everyone." self-love is such a rich emotion to possess. it's something that cannot be stripped away from you by anybody, except for you. that statement alone is empowering. in a world where nothing is promised, you can always have love for yourself.

Acknowledgements:

Thank you to my dearest friend **Molly** for bringing my idea for this book cover to life and doing it so beautifully. Molly, your support over the years has been incredibly vital to me, I would have given up a long time ago if it wasn't for you. You are an amazing artist, and I am so honored to be friends with someone so magnificent and talented. You always believed in me, even when I didn't, and for that I am forever grateful.

MKS, SM, CF, JR -
Thank you for your encouragement throughout this process, for being my support system, and for showing me what true friendship means. My heart is overflowing with love from you and for you, you all mean the world to me.

A special thank you to **You** for choosing to read my words. Amongst these pages are the etchings from my once broken heart. It took me years to gain the courage to share them with the world, and I appreciate you for giving me a chance.
I hope you remember to always put yourself first. You deserve to be the most important person in your own life.

Hold on to hope, sometimes it can be the only thing that saves you.